TODAY'S TOP DRIVERS

BUBBA WALLACE

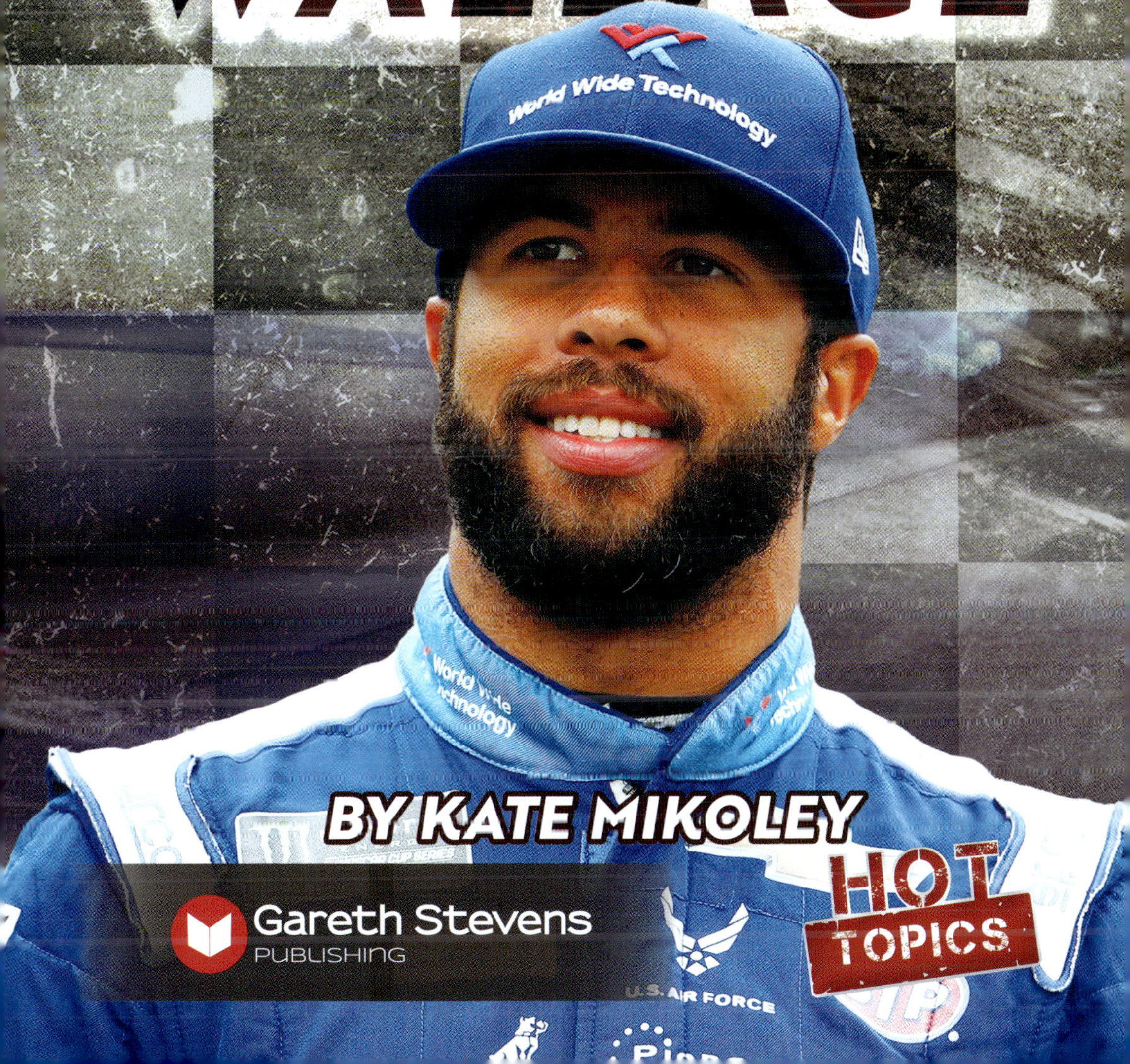

BY KATE MIKOLEY

Gareth Stevens PUBLISHING

HOT TOPICS

Please visit our website, www.garethstevens.com. For a free color catalog of all our high-quality books, call toll free 1-800-542-2595 or fax 1-877-542-2596.

Library of Congress Cataloging-in-Publication Data
Names: Mikoley, Kate, author.
Title: Bubba Wallace / Kate Mikoley.
Description: Buffalo, New York : Gareth Stevens Publishing, [2024] | Series: Today's top drivers | Includes bibliographical references and index.
Identifiers: LCCN 2023006874 (print) | LCCN 2023006875 (ebook) | ISBN 9781538287088 (library binding) | ISBN 9781538287071 (paperback) | ISBN 9781538287095 (ebook)
Subjects: LCSH: Wallace, Bubba, 1993—Juvenile literature. | Automobile racing drivers–United States–Biography–Juvenile literature. | African American athletes–United States–Biography–Juvenile literature. | African American athletes–Political activity–History–21st century. | Racism in sports–Juvenile literature. | NASCAR (Association)–History.
Classification: LCC GV1032.W34 M55 2024 (print) | LCC GV1032.W34 (ebook) | DDC 796.72092 [B]–dc23/eng/20230306
LC record available at https://lccn.loc.gov/2023006874
LC ebook record available at https://lccn.loc.gov/2023006875

First Edition

Published in 2024 by
Gareth Stevens Publishing
2544 Clinton St
Buffalo, NY 14224

Designer: Tanya Dellaccio Keeney
Editor: Kate MIkoley

Photo credits: Series background Merydolla/Shutterstock.com; cover, pp. 1 (Bubba), 9, 13, 14, 15, 19, 21, 29 Grindstone Media Group/Shutterstock.com; p. 5 https://upload.wikimedia.org/wikipedia/commons/d/d0/Bubba_Wallace_Driver_Introductions_Pocono_2022.jpg; p. 7 Charlie Neibergall/AP Images; p. 11 https://upload.wikimedia.org/wikipedia/commons/c/c7/Darrell_Wallace_Jr_Kyle_Busch_Motorsports_Toyota_Rockingham_2013.jpg; p. 17 (top) Georgia Peanut Commission/Flickr.com; p. 17 (bottom) https://upload.wikimedia.org/wikipedia/en/4/40/WendellScottRetiredNASCARDriver.jpg; p. 23 Steve Helber/AP Images; p. 25 Bruce Alan Bennett/Shutterstock.com; p. 27 Kathy Hutchins/Shutterstock.com.

Printed in the United States of America

CPSIA compliance information: Batch #CS24GS: For further information contact Gareth Stevens, New York, New York at 1-800-542-2595.

CONTENTS

FROM THE BEGINNING

Bubba Wallace is one of the most well-known race car drivers. But before he was famous, he was a kid in Concord, North Carolina, who loved racing. Today, he does more than just race. He also makes a difference in the sport he loves!

IN THE FAST LANE

Wallace was born on October 8, 1993, in Mobile, Alabama. His family later moved to Concord, where he was raised.

Bubba's full name is William Darrell Wallace Jr. He is named after his father, who owns a cleaning company. His mother is named Desiree. He also has a sister named Brittany. Bubba started racing when he was just 9 years old.

BUBBA AND HIS MOM, DESIREE

IN THE FAST LANE

Wallace's family gave him the nickname "Bubba" when he was a child.

EARLY WINS

As a kid, Wallace raced in the Bandolero **Series** and Legends Series. Both series use smaller **stock cars** made for younger drivers. He made a name for himself in 2005 when he won 35 of 48 races in the Bandolero Series!

IN THE FAST LANE

Wallace first made NASCAR history in 2010, when he won the first race in the K&N Pro Series East. He became the youngest and first Black driver to win a race in that series.

As a teen, Wallace was part of NASCAR's Drive for Diversity. This effort tries to get women and people of color to take part in racing. Historically, the sport has been made up mainly of white men.

IN THE FAST LANE

In 2013, Wallace won his first NASCAR Truck Series race. It had been 50 years since a Black driver won a race in one of NASCAR's top three national touring series!

GOING BIG

In 2018, Wallace started driving full-time in NASCAR's Cup Series. This is the premier, or top, series in the sport. He was the first Black driver to race full-time in the series in 47 years. That year, he came in second in the Daytona 500.

IN THE FAST LANE

In 2018, Wallace drove for Richard Petty Motorsports. He drove the team's No. 43 car.

A NEW TEAM

For the 2021 NASCAR season, basketball star Michael Jordan and NASCAR driver Denny Hamlin started their own team. Wallace was the first driver signed, or added, to the team, 23XI Racing.

MICHAEL JORDAN

IN THE FAST LANE

During his basketball* career*, Michael Jordan wore the No. 23 on his uniform. Wallace drives the No. 23 car for 23XI.

On October 4, 2021, Wallace won his first Cup Series race. The race was the YellaWood 500 at the Talladega Superspeedway. The win was also the first for 23XI Racing. It had been 58 years since a Black driver won a race in the premier series.

WENDELL SCOTT

IN THE FAST LANE

Wallace was just the second Black driver to win a race in NASCAR's top series. The first was Wendell Scott, in 1963.

Wallace won his second premier series race in 2022 at the Kansas Speedway. The race was the Hollywood Casino 400. The same year, he came in second place at the Daytona 500 again. The winner beat him by only 0.036 second!

IN THE FAST LANE

Wallace drove 23XI Racing's No. 45 Toyota in the 2022 Hollywood Casino 400.

A VOICE FOR CHANGE

As of 2022, Wallace is the only full-time Black driver in NASCAR. He is open about the **racism** he has faced in racing since he was a kid. Today, Wallace fights for equality and **inclusion** in NASCAR.

IN THE FAST LANE

Wallace tries to use the attention he receives for good. He has said he will "just keep fighting the good fight for me and continue to stand up for what I believe in."

In 2020, Wallace called on NASCAR to ban the Confederate flag from its events. The flag, used by the South in the American Civil War (1861-1865), is considered a racist sign. For a long time, it was commonly seen at races. In June 2020, NASCAR banned it.

IN THE FAST LANE

Wallace is active in the Black Lives Matter movement. In 2020, he drove a car that had messages from the movement on it.

TAKING RESPONSIBILITY

NASCAR is risky, so drivers sometimes get suspended, or banned for a time, if they do something that could cause harm. In 2022, NASCAR suspended Wallace from one race. Another driver hit Wallace's car. Then Wallace hit their car and later pushed the other driver.

IN THE FAST LANE

Wallace said he was sorry for his actions, stating, "My **behavior** does not [line up] with the [main] values that are shared by 23XI Racing and our partners."

OFF THE TRACK

Wallace started his own **charity** in 2017, the Live to Be Different Foundation. Its purpose is to show young people they can do anything they set their mind to and push them to be better than those before them.

IN THE FAST LANE

Each year, Wallace gives one male and one female student from his high school in North Carolina a $5,000 ***scholarship.***

LOOKING FORWARD

Wallace is still early in his career, but he's already doing great things—from winning races to standing up for what is right and helping others. With the future ahead of him, only time will tell what this top driver will do!

IN THE FAST LANE

In the 2022 season, Wallace had five top-five finishes.

TIMELINE

OCTOBER 8, 1993

WALLACE IS BORN.

2005

HE WINS 35 OF 48 RACES IN THE BANDOLERO SERIES.

2010

WALLACE WINS THE K&N PRO SERIES EAST.

2013

WALLACE WINS HIS FIRST NASCAR TRUCK SERIES RACE.

2018

HE STARTS DRIVING FULL-TIME IN NASCAR'S CUP SERIES.

2020

NASCAR BANS THE CONFEDERATE FLAG, WITH A PUSH FROM WALLACE.

2021

WALLACE STARTS DRIVING FOR 23XI RACING.

HE WINS HIS FIRST CUP SERIES RACE.

2022

WALLACE WINS THE HOLLYWOOD CASINO 400.

FOR MORE INFORMATION

BOOKS

Abdo, Kenny. *Bubba Wallace.* Minneapolis, MN: Fly!, 2022.

Crayton, Lisa A. *Bubba Wallace: Stock Car Racing Star.* North Mankato, MN: Capstone Press, 2022.

Stratton, Connor. *Bubba Wallace: Auto Racing Star.* Lake Elmo, MN: Focus Readers, 2021.

WEBSITES

Bubba Wallace
www.bubbawallace.com/
Learn more about Bubba Wallace on his website.

Bubba Wallace: NASCAR Driver Page
www.nascar.com/drivers/bubba-wallace
Find Wallace's latest race stats on his NASCAR driver page.

Toyota Racing: Bubba Wallace
www.toyota.com/racing/nascar-cup/drivers/bubba-wallace
This page has the latest news about Bubba's races.

GLOSSARY

behavior: The way someone acts.

career: The job someone chooses to do for a long time.

charity: A group that helps those in need.

inclusion: The act of including people of all backgrounds.

racism: The belief that people of different races have different qualities and abilities and that some are better than others.

scholarship: Money awarded to help someone pay for their education.

series: A set of events or races that go together.

stock car: A racing car that looks similar to a regular car.

INDEX